Cornerstones of Freedom

The Story of

THE

BOSTON

TEA PARTY

By R. Conrad Stein

Illustrated by Keith Neely

 CHILDRENS PRESS, CHICAGO

Library of Congress Cataloging in Publication Data

Stein, R. Conrad.
    The story of the Boston Tea Party.

    (Cornerstones of freedom)
    Summary: Recounts the events leading up to the colo-
nists' defiant act against the British known as the Boston
Tea Party, which ultimately climaxed in the American
Revolution.
    1. Boston Tea Party, 1773—Juvenile literature.
[1. Boston Tea Party, 1773. 2. United States—History—
Revolution, 1775-1783—Causes] I. Neely, Keith,
1943- ill. II. Title. III. Series.
E215.7.S84   1984   973.3'115   83-27319
ISBN 0-516-04666-7

On a wintry afternoon in Boston, some school children began to play their favorite game. The object of the game was to provoke a British soldier. The children especially enjoyed making fun of the bright red coat that was part of the British Army uniform.

"Bloodyback, Bloodyback," sang one boy at the lone sentry standing in front of the Custom House on King Street.

"Lobster, Lobster," jeered another.

Then a third boy packed a snowball and flung it at the soldier. The snowball thumped against the wooden door just inches from the sentry's head. The guard swore and shook his musket at the children. They scurried away, giggling. The few adults walking the sidewalk hid smiles. To Bostonians, the British troops stationed in their city were a hated occupying army.

5

Later that cold evening, bigger trouble brewed for the soldier standing guard on King Street. A teenaged boy who worked as a barber's apprentice also had taunted him. The enraged soldier had struck the boy with his musket and knocked him down. Soon afterward the boy returned with a sizable crowd of waterfront dockworkers. The sentry spotted the approaching crowd and shouted for help. He was quickly joined by a squad of troops commanded by a British captain named Preston.

The gang of workers stopped in front of the British troops and began cursing at them. Some threw pieces of ice. The red-coated soldiers readied their rifles. The workers, some of whom had been drinking whiskey, continued to harass the "redcoats." Captain Preston later testified that the crowd called out, "Come on you Rascals, you Bloodybacks, you Lobster Scoundrels; fire if you dare." Captain Preston told his men to remain calm. He then shouted to the workers, commanding them to go home. But the crowd of angry, yelling Bostonians grew in number.

Then tragedy struck. Later, no one could agree on exactly what had gone wrong. Perhaps a nervous finger jerked a trigger. Or perhaps Captain Preston

tried to restrain his troops by shouting, "Don't fire! Don't fire!" and one excited redcoat heard only the word *fire*. Whatever the cause, a musket flashed in the twilight. The first crack was followed by another and then another. When the gunsmoke had cleared, five members of the crowd lay dead or dying in the slush of King Street.

The incident occurred on March 5, 1770. Ever since, for more than two centuries of American history, it has been called "The Boston Massacre."

The Boston Massacre was one of many clashes that broke out between colonists and British authorities before the Revolutionary War. The reasons for the friction between the colonies and the mother country were many and complicated.

At the time of the Boston Massacre, the British had already been in North America for 150 years. Starting with their first tiny settlement at Jamestown, British colonists spread up and down the Atlantic seaboard. By 1770 they numbered more than two million. Most of the colonists had strong ties to the British Isles and were doggedly loyal to the Crown. Over the years, British rule had been fair. The government in London allowed the colonies to establish their own local governments and pass their own laws. Until the 1760s few colonists dreamed of declaring their land independent from Great Britain. Even when the Revolutionary War broke out, historians estimate that only about one-third of the colonial people favored independence. Another third of the colonists were neutral on the subject. And the final third stubbornly wanted to remain subjects of Great Britain.

The good relations between the colonies and the mother country first began to break down after the long and bitter French and Indian War. The war ended in 1763, a stunning victory by the British over the French and their Indian allies. Great Britain, the mighty lion, now ruled over most of North America. But the war had cost a great deal of money. Great Britain was deeply in debt. Since the British people were already overtaxed, the king turned to his prize colonies to pay some of the war bills. Britain imposed a series of new taxes on America. One of these was a tax on stamps.

The tax on stamps had a brief but dramatic impact on American history. Enacted in 1765, the Stamp Act required colonists to buy stamps to put on legal documents such as deeds, licenses, school diplomas, and mortgage agreements. The colonists were outraged by this form of taxation. Tax collectors were beaten up and shot at. A boycott halted the buying of British-made goods in the colonies. A special Stamp Act Congress met in New York to protest the law.

Shocked by the colonists' reaction, Britain's Parliament met in 1766 and voted to repeal the Stamp Act. The American rebellion might have ended right there, but Parliament insisted that the colonists were still English subjects and that the government, therefore, had the right to tax them. The colonists disagreed. Certainly English citizens living in the mother country could be taxed by their government. They had representatives in Parliament to fight for their rights if the taxes became severe. But the American colonists had no such representatives in Parliament. So, they argued, they should not be taxed. The slogan "Taxation without representation is tyranny" echoed throughout the colonies.

Still the British Parliament passed laws imposing taxes on the colonies. In 1767 Parliament passed the Townshend Acts, which placed a tax on lead, paint, paper, and tea. Once more the colonists raised a storm of protest. And once more Parliament repealed the taxes on all the items except, significantly, the tax on tea.

Americans had acquired the habit of tea-drinking from the British. Tea was their favorite beverage. Because tea was so important to colonial life, its tax was particularly aggravating. With every pot of tea brewed, a colonist anguished over the taxes.

Resistance to the new taxes had the profound effect of uniting the colonies. In the past, colonists had thought of themselves first as Pennsylvanians, Virginians, or New Yorkers. Rivalries and even hatreds between colonies were common. But suddenly all thirteen colonies faced a common enemy in the tax-hungry British government. As South Carolina's Christopher Gadsden told a gathering of colonists, "There ought to be no more New England men, no New Yorkers...but all of us Americans."

Because of the violence of the American opposition to taxation, the British Parliament decided to send troops to the colonies. The city of Boston was a hotbed of anti-British activities. So, in 1768, a British fleet landed at that city and four thousand red-coated soldiers disembarked. Bostonians felt betrayed. All their lives they had believed they were English subjects, loyal to the Crown. But as they watched the redcoats marching through the streets of their city, they suddenly felt like a conquered people.

Stationing troops in Boston was an invitation to disaster, a disaster that occurred with the Boston Massacre. Actually, the massacre was really little more than a tragic street fight. History probably would have forgotten the incident had it not been for the efforts of an energetic anti-British Bostonian named Samuel Adams.

Sam Adams was born in Boston in 1722. He was a

SAMUEL ADAMS

distant cousin to John Adams, who was to become the second president of the United States. Sam Adams grew up in a comfortable middle-class home, graduated from Harvard, and entered the business world, where he failed miserably. He was constantly late for appointments, his clothes were disheveled, and he had no mind for details. So Adams turned to politics, where he enjoyed a smashing success.

If he were alive today, Sam Adams could probably run a successful political campaign for a presidential candidate. He was not a great public speaker. But he was an excellent speech writer, with a keen sense of how to excite an audience. Historian Samuel Eliot Morison said of Sam Adams, "He was certainly the western world's first orchestra leader of revolution. He knew that voters are moved by their emotions rather than by logic."

Like a panther springing on its prey, Sam Adams pounced on the Boston Massacre episode. His skillfully written pamphlets turned the street fight on King Street into a deliberate slaughter. The unemployed dockworkers who were shot at by panicky troops became noble patriots cruelly cut down by redcoat tyrants. Adams was aided in spreading his version of the events in Boston by a picture that was printed up and circulated throughout the colonies. The picture had been drawn by another anti-British Bostonian, silversmith Paul Revere. It showed British troops coldly firing on an unarmed and seemingly innocent gathering of people.

The tireless Sam Adams waged a campaign aimed at turning loyal colonists' feelings against British

rule. A master of propaganda, he organized dances around a stately old elm tree in Boston Common, a tree called the Liberty Tree. He taught people the words to a new liberty song, which had a lively tune that anyone, even the poorest of singers, could bawl out. He organized chapters of the Sons of Liberty, a secret society that met to discuss the overthrow of British rule in the colonies.

Still, Adams was slow to convince his fellow colonists to sever the bonds that connected them to

Great Britain. For a century and a half, the colonies and the mother country had been a happy family. Despite the new taxes and the bloodshed in Boston, few colonists wanted a family squabble. Besides, the British had demonstrated that they were willing to compromise on taxes. Most of the new taxes had been repealed by the British government after the American protests.

Most of the taxes had been repealed—except, as Sam Adams delighted in pointing out, the tax on tea.

Actually, the British tea tax cost a colonial family only pennies a year. Still, it was a tax that could be raised or lowered at the will of Parliament. Every colonist knew the truth of a statement later uttered by a famous American judge: "The power to tax is the power to destroy."

In 1773 the British Parliament used its power to tax. Parliament rigged the tax system to give the British-owned East India Company a monopoly over tea sold to the colonies. "Outrageous and damnable!" shouted American merchants. Businessmen in the colonies were highly independent and hated monopolies. Also, the new tax system made it impossible for anyone other than an agent of the East India Company to profit from the tea trade. All over the colonies, people fumed at the new tea-tax laws. And in Boston, Sam Adams sprang into action.

Adams held meetings with other anti-British radicals. Just a partial list of those radical Bostonians reads like a roll call of leaders of the American Revolution. There was John Adams, an enemy of the British and a future United States president. There was John Hancock, Boston's wealthiest merchant and a man who later scrawled a larger-than-life signature on the Declaration of Independence so that

JOHN ADAMS

JOHN HANCOCK

JOSEPH WARREN

PAUL REVERE

the British king could read it without the aid of glasses. Another member of the group was Dr. Joseph Warren, a fearless radical, who was later killed in the Battle of Bunker Hill. And there was Paul Revere, a master silversmith, a splendid horseman, and a determined enemy of British rule.

The radical Bostonians carried their protest against the tea tax to the Governor of Massachusetts. At the time, Thomas Hutchinson served as the colony's royal governor. Like all royal governors, Hutchinson had been appointed to his office by the British government. Though he was born in America, Hutchinson's sympathies were with the British king. He considered the radicals to be trouble-making criminals. The radicals, in turn, accused Hutchinson of making a profit from his pro-British stand. Sam Adams, who loved to pour fuel on controversial fires, pointed out that two of the agents chosen by the East India Company to sell tea in Massachusetts were Governor Hutchinson's sons.

Governor Hutchinson ignored the letters of protest sent to his office by the radicals. He insisted that all tea arriving in the Boston Harbor would be subject to the full British tax.

In September of 1773, the radicals learned that three British ships carrying cargoes of tea were heading for Boston under full sail. Sam Adams and his friends knew that if those ships unloaded at the harbor and the king's tax was paid, the radicals' cause would be lost. Even one payment of the hated tea tax would be a crushing defeat.

The radicals next turned their efforts against the newly appointed agents of the East India Company. These men, mostly colonists born in America, were pro-British in their politics. At one o'clock in the morning, members of the Sons of Liberty banged on the doors of five Boston agents of the East India Company. The Sons of Liberty members handed each of the agents a summons demanding that he meet with the townspeople at the Liberty Tree the next day at noon. The summons said the purpose of the meeting was "... to make a public resignation of your commission."

The next morning, handbills were nailed up on nearly every door in Boston urging the citizens to attend the meeting at the Liberty Tree. At the bottom of each handbill was a bold Sons of Liberty warning, "Show me the man that dare take this down." At noon a crowd of five hundred had gathered beneath the Liberty Tree. Leading the townspeople were Sam Adams, Dr. Joseph Warren, and John Hancock. The colonists hoped to watch the agents of the East India Company publicly resign from their jobs. A riot nearly broke out when the agents failed to appear. Finally tempers cooled and the crowd disbanded.

Meanwhile, the ships carrying the East India Company tea sailed ever closer to the Boston Harbor.

In the next few weeks, more mass meetings were held. In speech after speech, orators denounced the tea tax as "British tyranny." Many colonists quit their lifelong tea-drinking habit. Coffee, which many substituted for tea, got its start as a popular beverage in America.

On a gray Sunday afternoon, November 18, 1773, the tea ship *Dartmouth* sailed into Boston Harbor. Hours later, handbills passed furiously from one Bostonian to another: "Friends! Brethren! Countrymen! That worst of plagues, the detested tea, shipped for this port by the East India Company, is now arrived in this harbor. Every friend of this country. . . is now called upon to meet, to make a united and successful resistance."

In the meeting, townspeople demanded that the *Dartmouth* be sent directly back to England with the tea still in her hold. But Governor Hutchinson insisted that the tea the *Dartmouth* carried be unloaded and that the ship's owner pay every penny of the tax levied by the British Crown. However, the Governor feared that angry Bostonians would riot if crewmen tried to unload the ship. So the *Dartmouth* remained tied up at the Boston wharf. All her cargo except her chests of tea was taken off. As the days passed, two more tea ships—the *Eleanor* and the *Beaver*—also arrived at the Boston Harbor. They, too, tied up at the waterfront, but the crews did not remove the tea chests from their holds.

Tension gripped all of Boston. Abigail Adams described the mood of the city well when she wrote to her husband John: "The flame is kindled and like lightning it catches from soul to soul." Governor Hutchinson said, "The town is as furious as it was in the time of the Stamp Act."

Finally, Governor Hutchinson set a deadline. He ordered the *Dartmouth* to be unloaded by December 17, 1773. If the radicals interfered with the unloading, he said, they would have to answer to the British Army.

The largest mass meeting in Boston's history took place on the evening of December 16. Some seven thousand people gathered at Boston's Old South Meeting House. Fiery speeches were made. The crowd's mood was angry. Then Sam Adams took the floor and uttered one sentence: "This meeting can do nothing more to save the country."

Adams' words were like a trigger. Shouts came from the crowd: "The Boston Harbor will be a teapot tonight!" "Who knows how tea will mingle with salt water?" "Hurrah for the Mohawks!"

What happened next is well-known. Exactly why it happened is shrouded in mystery. Many historians believe that Sam Adams' statement—"This meeting can do nothing more to save the country"—was a prearranged signal to set in motion a well-laid plan. Other historians believe the events of that night were more spontaneous. Whatever the motives, about a hundred men stormed out of the meeting hall, disguised themselves as Mohawk Indians, and marched to the waterfront. The famous Boston Tea Party had begun.

The participants in the Boston Tea Party intended to dump the disputed tea overboard. They hoped to do this in an orderly way without violence. And they succeeded brilliantly. However, the men were engaged in an illegal act against the British government. If apprehended, they could be put to death. It was for that reason they disguised themselves as Indians. Also the "Mohawks" who actually dumped the tea kept their participation in the Boston Tea Party a secret for years to come. Only after the Revolutionary War did some of them give written accounts of their actions on that historic night.

At the waterfront, the supposed Mohawks were divided into three groups and leaders were selected. Each group boarded a different tea ship. The ships' captains, facing such a large mob, had no choice but to give the men the keys to their cargo holds.

One of the disguised participants was a sixteen-year-old apprentice blacksmith named Joshua Wyeth. Years later he wrote: "Our leader, in a stern and resolute manner, ordered the captain and crew to open the hatchways and hand us the hoisting tackle and ropes. The captain asked what we intended to do. Our leader told him we were going to unload the tea, and ordered him and the crew below. They instantly obeyed.

"Some of our number then jumped into the hold, and passed the chests to the tackle. As they were hauled on deck, others knocked them open with axes. Others raised them to the railing and discharged their contents overboard."

With axes striking and cranes creaking, the work went on. The ships' crewmen made no attempt to interfere with the tea dumping. In fact, to the

astonishment of the Mohawks, a few British sailors even helped the colonists.

A large crowd of Bostonians gathered at the wharf to watch. Seeing all that valuable, tasty tea being dumped over the side was too painful for some of them. As a Mohawk named George Hewes recalled, "During the time we were throwing tea overboard, there were several attempts made by some of the citizens to carry off small quantities of it for their family use.... One [man] whom I well knew, came on board for that purpose, and when he supposed he was not noticed, filled his pockets, and also the lining of his coat [with tea]. But I had detected him and gave information to the leader of what he was doing. We were ordered to take him into custody, [but] he made his escape. He had, however, to run a gauntlet through the crowd upon the wharf, each one, as he passed, giving him a kick."

It took a little more than two hours to split open the 342 chests of tea aboard the three ships and spill the contents overboard. When finished, the leaders returned the cargo-hold keys to the ships' captains. Then the raiders manned brooms and swept the decks clean. There had been no violence. The only casualty of the night came when a Bostonian named John Crane was knocked unconscious by a swinging derrick. He later walked home nursing a headache.

"We were surrounded by British armed ships, but no attempt was made to resist us," wrote George Hewes. The British warships anchored nearby bristled with guns, but could not fire without destroying much of the harbor. And the work was completed so efficiently and so swiftly that the British Army had no time to interfere.

The Mohawks waved good-bye to the ships' captains and crewmen and formed a double line at the wharf. Tea leaves covered the choppy water for hundreds of yards around the three ships. At the command "Shoulder arms!" the Mohawks placed their axes on their shoulders and marched away from the waterfront. Onlookers cheered the marching men. Someone in the column played a merry tune on a fife. Broad grins lit the faces of the young marchers. They were only simple townsmen, but that night they had twisted the tail of the mighty British lion.

Paul Revere, the best horseman in Boston, galloped off to other colonies to spread the news of the tea dumping. Radicals everywhere applauded the brave Bostonians. Just days after the Boston Tea Party, taverns from Virginia to New Hampshire rang with a new song:

> Rally, Mohawks! bring out your axes,
> And tell King George we'll pay no taxes
>   On his foreign tea.

The events in Boston infuriated the king and the British Parliament. Parliament decided to act ruthlessly, even though the members knew they could push their prize colonies into rebellion. In London, Lord North said, "We must risk something, if we do not it is all over." Parliament sent more troops, closed the Port of Boston, and put the city under a form of martial law.

The actions punishing Boston served only to

further unite the colonies. Speakers in town meetings up and down the Atlantic coast declared a new loyalty. As the radical Patrick Henry shouted to an assembly, "The distinctions between Virginians, Pennsylvanians, New Yorkers, New Englanders are no more. I am not a Virginian, but an American."

The Boston Tea Party was a heroic act of protest by a weak colonial people against the greatest power on earth. At the Boston Harbor, on December 16, 1773, David had defied Goliath. Speaking of that night, John Adams wrote in his diary, "This is the most magnificent movement of all. There is a Dignity, a Majesty, a Sublimity in this last Effort of the Patriots that I greatly admire. . . . This destruction of the Tea is so bold, so daring, so firm, intrepid and inflexible, and it must have so important consequences, and so lasting, that I cannot but consider it as an Epoch in History."

Many historians call the Boston Tea Party the start of the American Revolution. After the tea dumping, events leading to war with the mother country snowballed. Sixteen months later, a ragtag American army engaged the British regulars at the towns of Lexington and Concord. A long war had begun. And a new nation was born.

About the Author

R. Conrad Stein was born and grew up in Chicago. He enlisted in the Marine Corps at the age of eighteen and served for three years. He then attended the University of Illinois where he received a Bachelor's degree in history. He later studied in Mexico, earning an advanced degree from the University of Guanajuato. Mr. Stein is the author of many other books, articles, and short stories written for young people.

Mr. Stein is married to Deborah Kent, who is also a writer of books for young readers.

About the Artist

Keith Neely attended the School of the Art Institute of Chicago and received a Bachelor of Fine Arts degree with honors from the Art Center College of Design, where he majored in illustration. He has worked as an art director, designer, and illustrator and has taught advertising illustration and advertising design at Biola College in La Mirada, California. Mr. Neely is currently a freelance illustrator whose work has appeared in numerous magazines, books, and advertisements. He lives in Florida with his wife and five children.